Intangible Asset Valuation

Steven M. Bragg

AccountingTools®

ISBN 978-1-64221-275-4

For more information about AccountingTools® products, visit our Web site at www.accountingtools.com.

Table of Contents

About the Author

Steven Bragg, CPA, has been the chief financial officer or controller of four companies, as well as a consulting manager at Ernst & Young. He received a master's degree in finance from Bentley College, an MBA from Babson College, and a Bachelor's degree in Economics from the University of Maine. He has been a two-time president of the Colorado Mountain Club, and is an avid alpine skier, mountain biker, and certified master diver. Mr. Bragg resides in Centennial, Colorado. He has written more than 300 books and courses, including *New Controller Guidebook*, *GAAP Guidebook*, and *Payroll Management*.

Steven maintains the accountingtools.com web site, which contains continuing professional education courses, the Accounting Best Practices podcast, and thousands of articles on accounting subjects.

Chapter 1
Overview of Intangible Assets

Introduction

A large part of the competitive advantage of a business may be due to its intangible assets, rather than its physical ones. What is an intangible asset, and how can it be valued? In this chapter, we cover the nature of this asset class, list examples of them, and provide an overview of the methods that can be used to assign values to them.

What is an Intangible Asset?

Intangible assets are assets that have no physical substance, where their value is derived from their associated legal rights. For example, the value of a broadcasting license is the legal right to keep anyone else from using the associated radio frequency. Or, the value of a patent is that its holder can prevent anyone else from exploiting the related concept. An intangible asset should produce some sort of value for its owner, perhaps in the form of an incremental gain in sales or a reduction in costs, or perhaps by increasing the value of other assets held by the business. For example, the owner of a taxi license could rent it out, resulting in an inflow of rental payments.

EXAMPLE

Milford Sound obtains a trademark for its Reverberate line of speakers. The company president then decides not to use the trademark to defend the trade name. In this case, because the trademark is never used to defend the trade name, it has minimal economic value to the business, because it is not being used. Given these facts, it would be difficult to assign a value to the asset.

EXAMPLE

Milford Sound has developed proprietary software that configures its speaker systems for the rooms in which they are placed. The value of the software is the incremental increase in value that it creates for the company's speakers.

In addition, an intangible asset must be specifically recognizable, be documented through some manifestation of its existence (such as a license, contract, permit, or drawing), and have come into existence as a result of a specific event. For example, a patent is an intangible asset because there is a specific patent registration document associated with it, as issued by the United States Patent and Trademark Office. Or, a listing of customers provides evidence that a business has a customer relationships intangible asset associated with the list. As another example, an intangible asset associated with some form of proprietary technology may be proven with blueprints, flowcharts, procedure manuals, and so forth. Finally, an intangible asset should be subject to private ownership, which means that it should be sellable to a third party. This does not mean that there has to be an active secondary market for the asset, only that it is possible to transfer it to someone else. For example, there is no active secondary market for the sale of book copyrights, but it is still possible to transfer this asset to a third party. In short, there are several features that should be present before you can legitimately recognize an intangible asset.

> **Note:** An intangible asset is considered to be transferrable to a third party even when it is customarily only transferred as part of a larger bundle of assets.

In addition, there are a variety of intangible factors that may contribute to the value of an intangible asset, but which are not intangible assets themselves. For example, being in a monopoly position is not an intangible asset, though it certainly contributes to the profitability of the business. Or, having a competitive edge over the competition does not by itself constitute an intangible asset, though the processes that create this advantage may be considered intangible assets. Further, being considered trustworthy by customers is certainly a contributor to overall corporate value, but this condition is not considered an intangible asset. While none of these factors are intangible assets, they are indicators that actual intangible assets exist.

Conversely, it can also be useful to define what is *not* an intangible asset. A *tangible asset* is any asset from which its value is derived from the use of its physical attributes. For example, the value of production machinery is derived from the ability of that machinery to produce parts, while the value of a building is derived from its occupancy.

Examples of Intangible Assets

So far, we have discussed the characteristics of intangible assets, but have not provided examples of the types of intangible assets that a business is most likely to encounter. Here are several examples:

Marketing-related intangible assets

- Trademarks[1]
- Service marks
- Trade dress[2]
- Newspaper mastheads
- Internet domain names
- Noncompetition agreements

---

[1] A trademark links goods to a specific manufacturer, while a service mark links services to a specific producer.
[2] Trade dress is the design and shape of the materials in which a product is packaged (such as a Coca-Cola bottle).

Customer-related intangible assets

- Customer lists
- Subscription lists
- Order backlog
- Customer relationships
- Distribution networks
- Loan portfolios

Artistic-related intangible assets

- Performance events
- Literary works (copyrights)[3]
- Musical works
- Pictures
- Motion pictures and television programs

Contract-based intangible assets

- Customer contracts
- Supplier contracts
- Licensing agreements
- Service contracts
- Lease agreements
- Franchise agreements
- Broadcast rights
- Regulatory approvals
- Royalty agreements
- Employment contracts

Property-based intangible assets

- Airport gate leases
- Docking rights
- Drilling rights
- Environmental rights
- Mining rights
- Property leases
- Property use rights
- Rights of way
- Surface rights
- Use rights (such as drilling rights or water rights)
- Water rights

---

[3] A copyright provides a specific right to produce an authored work.

Intellectual property-based intangible assets

- Patents
- Copyrighted authored works
- Trademarks
- Trade secrets (such as secret formulas and recipes)[4]

Intellectual property differs from other types of intangible assets, in that it is creatively and consciously produced, while other types of intangible property are naturally created as part of the process of running a business. Thus, an order backlog is created as part of the process of running a business, while the development of software is a deliberate and conscious act. Also, it is generally easier to sell off intellectual property, since it usually has specifically-transferrable legal ownership rights. This is not the case for more general types of intangible property, such as customer contracts or customer relationships.

Another intangible asset is goodwill, which is recognized by an acquirer as part of an acquisition. *Goodwill* is the difference between the price paid for an acquiree and the fair value of all assets and liabilities of the acquiree that were purchased as part of the business combination. In essence, goodwill is the excess paid over the amount that should have been paid just for identifiable assets and liabilities.

The Useful Life of an Intangible Asset

The intent of many owners of intangible property is that the property will have an infinite lifespan, if properly maintained. It is more likely that this property will eventually decline in value, or cease having any value at all. In many cases, the termination date of an intangible asset can be predicted with some accuracy. For example, a patent has a firm expiration date, as does a copyright, an operating license, and a contract. Or, you might be planning to replace it with a newer asset. A less predictable termination date occurs when a court or regulatory entity changes the rules or laws upon which an intangible asset is based, at which point it loses all value. For example, a taxi license has little value if the municipality that granted it decides to no longer regulate the number of taxis on its streets.

When to Conduct an Intangible Asset Valuation

There are several reasons why a business might conduct an intangible asset valuation. Here are some of the more common reasons:

- When determining the price at which an intangible asset will be sold
- When setting a price at which intellectual property will be licensed
- When establishing the ownership interest in a business to which intellectual property is being contributed
- When initially determining the recognized value of an intangible asset

---

[4] A trade secret is a secret device or technique used to manufacture products.

- When determining whether there has been an impairment of intangible asset value
- When setting the insured value of an intangible asset
- When transferring intangible assets between corporate subsidiaries
- When allocating the purchased price of a business among its various assets and liabilities
- When valuing the assets of a business that has emerged from bankruptcy
- When setting transfer prices for the transfer of intangible assets between subsidiaries

From an accounting perspective, the most common reasons to conduct intangible asset valuations are to assign values to the assets acquired from another entity as part of an acquisition, or to review asset values as part of a periodic impairment analysis.

Methods for Deriving the Value of Intangible Assets

There are several approaches available for deriving the value of an intangible asset. The correct one to use will depend on the nature of the asset and the availability of information. Your choices are as follows:

- *Fair value.* A common valuation method involves the determination of what a willing purchaser would be willing to pay for an asset in an orderly transaction between market participants.
- *Market price.* A valuation approach frequently applied to intangible assets is the determination of market price, which is the most likely price at which an asset would be sold in an open market.

The preceding two approaches can be difficult to apply to the valuation of an intangible asset, since there may be no market or record of similar transactions from which a fair market value can be derived. If so, consider using one of the following methods instead:

- *Acquisition value.* This is the greatest price that a specific buyer would be willing to pay for an intangible asset. This derivation will vary depending on the targeted buyer, and so can potentially result in a significant range of values.
- *Specific use value.* This is the price that a buyer would be willing to pay for an intangible asset for a specific use (which is not necessarily its highest and best use). Depending on the proposed application, this can result in a significantly lower valuation than the outcome derived from other methods.

If several of these valuation methods were to be used, it is quite possible that the outcome would be a relatively broad range of values, since each one is based on different inputs. If so, it will be necessary to reconcile the various outcomes and arrive at a single value. The first step in this reconciliation is to review the entire valuation process to see if it has been performed correctly, and using the right assumptions.

Specifically, you should evaluate the different methods used based on the following issues:

- How available was the data? In some cases, there may be vast amounts of publicly-available data that can be used for a valuation analysis. Conversely, data may be extremely hard to come by in other industries.
- How much data was available for making valuation decisions, and what was the quality level of the data? A quality valuation cannot be achieved without being based on a sufficient amount of high-quality data.
- Were there any legal or contractual issues impacting the asset? For example, the IRS may mandate that a certain valuation method be applied when determining a valuation for tax purposes.
- What is the industry in which the asset is used? If an asset is used across several industries, the valuation method applied to it may vary by industry. This customary usage may influence the valuation method chosen.
- What rights were associated with the asset? The value of an asset may be impacted by the rights associated with it, such as usage rights that have been granted to a third party.
- What was the nature of the asset? Depending on the asset, there may be accepted valuation standards (such as $1 million valuation for the lease on an airport gate), which may be useful for verifying a derived value.

Once these issues have been addressed, you will be in a better position to arrive at a single, synthesized value for the asset in question. A reasonable approach for doing so is to create a weighted average valuation, where an increased weighting is given to whichever valuation approach was based on more reliable and available data (which is a judgment call for the analyst). It may be useful to write a short narrative that explains the reasons for the weighting, in case the valuation is audited.

EXAMPLE

Gatekeeper Corporation (an operator of toll roads) acquires a similar business, and wants to develop a valuation for the automated toll management software of its new subsidiary. It develops a valuation based on three different methods (as described in the following chapters), and assigns different weightings to each outcome. The average method is noted in the following table.

Valuation approach	Derived Value	Weighting Percentage	Weighted Value
Cost	$4,200,000	25%	$1,050,000
Market	4,700,000	50%	2,350,000
Income	5,000,000	25%	1,250,000
			$4,650,000

In the accompanying explanatory notes, the analyst points out that the market data was based on the sale of two quite similar software assets within the industry, and both within the past year. Given the relevance of this data, the analyst felt that a higher weighting should be accorded to the outcome of the market valuation method.

Ideally, a derived set of asset valuations will be tightly clustered around a single value. This is the ideal scenario, making it easier for the analyst to settle upon a single valuation figure. However, there will be other times when there will be a valuation outlier, perhaps where most of the values are tightly clustered, while another value is well away from these values. When an outlier arises, one should certainly investigate why the value differs so markedly from the other outcomes; doing so may reveal a flaw in the data or the method that can be corrected. If this investigation still results in an outlier valuation, then you will need to decide whether to throw it out or still include it in a weighted valuation, perhaps with a lower weighting. A low weighting might be justified if the underlying calculation appears to be correct, even though the valuation is unusually high or low.

Summary

The valuation of an intangible asset may be derived in a number of ways, as noted in this chapter and expanded upon in the following chapters. It can be difficult to pin an exact number on a valuation, so the analyst strives to assemble several outcomes from different valuation approaches, to see if the resulting numbers can be used to develop a single, defensible asset value. In the next chapter, we delve deeper into the fair value concept, to see how it can be applied to the valuation of intangible assets.

Chapter 2
Fair Value Analysis

Introduction

From the perspective of the accountant, the valuation of intangible assets is usually triggered by a business combination, where all of the assets and liabilities of the acquiree are recorded at their fair values. In this chapter, we provide examples of the types of intangible assets that may be recognized through a business combination, and then delve into how the fair values of these assets may be derived.

Fair Value in Business Combinations

When an organization acquires another entity, the acquirer should recognize identifiable assets and liabilities of the acquiree at their fair values as of the acquisition date. It is entirely possible that the acquirer will recognize assets and liabilities that the acquiree had never recorded in its own accounting records. In particular, the acquirer will likely assign fair values to a variety of intangible assets that the acquiree may have developed internally, and so was constrained by GAAP from recognizing as assets. Examples of these intangible assets are noted in the following table.

Examples of Intangible Assets

Broadcast rights	Internet domain names	Noncompetition agreements
Computer software	Lease agreements	Order backlog
Customer lists	Licensing agreements	Patented technology
Customer relationships	Literary works	Pictures
Employment contracts	Motion pictures	Service contracts
Franchise agreements	Musical works	Trademarks

The Fair Value Concept

Fair value is the estimated price at which an asset can be sold or a liability settled in an orderly transaction to a third party under current market conditions. This is a hypothetical transaction – there is no need to actually sell an asset or settle a liability. The definition of fair value includes the following concepts:

- *Current market conditions.* The derivation of fair value should be based on market conditions on the measurement date, rather than a transaction that occurred at some earlier date.
- *Intent.* The intention of the holder of an asset or liability to continue to hold it is irrelevant to the measurement of fair value. Such intent might otherwise alter the measured fair value. For example, if the intent is to immediately sell

an asset, this could be inferred to trigger a rushed sale, which may result in a lower sale price.

- *Orderly transaction*. Fair value is to be derived based on an orderly transaction, which infers a transaction where there is no undue pressure to sell. Undue pressure can arise, for example, in a corporate liquidation. This also implies that the counterparty is not being forced to acquire an asset or settle a liability.
- *Third party*. Fair value is to be derived based on a presumed sale to an entity that is not a corporate insider or related in any way to the seller. Otherwise, a related-party transaction might skew the price paid. In addition, a third party that may participate in a sale or settlement transaction should have a reasonable knowledge of the asset or liability in question, based on customary levels of due diligence.

The Active Market Concept

The ideal determination of fair value is based on prices offered in an active market. An *active market* is one in which there is a sufficiently high volume of transactions to provide ongoing pricing information. Also, the market from which a fair value is derived should be the principal market for the asset or liability, since the greater transaction volume associated with such a market should presumably lead to the best prices for the seller. The market in which a business normally sells the asset type in question or settles liabilities is assumed to be the principal market. Thus, the designation of a principal market is from the perspective of the reporting entity; a different market might be the principal market for a competitor.

> **Note:** If there is no principal market for the assets or liabilities being valued, the alternative is to obtain a fair value from the *most advantageous market*, which is the market in which the best price can be obtained, net of transaction costs.

Measuring Fair Value when Transaction Volume is Low

A company may rely upon the prices obtained in a particular market to derive its fair value calculations. These prices can require significant adjustment if the volume of activity in the market has declined. In such an environment, individual transaction prices could be well above or below what would be found if there were more willing buyers and sellers in the marketplace. Evidence of such a decline includes:

- A reduced number of recent transactions
- There are large swings in quoted prices, either over time or among market makers
- There is no longer a strong correlation between an index and the fair value of an asset or liability
- A wide bid-ask spread, or a notable increase in the spread
- There has been a decline in the market for new issuances
- There is little publicly-available information for related transactions

If there has been a decline in the volume of activity, transaction prices may still fairly reflect fair value. However, if these transactions no longer represent fair value, it will be necessary to adjust the transactions or quoted prices to arrive at a reasonable fair value measurement.

There is no prescribed methodology in GAAP for making this adjustment, though the market approach, cost approach, and income approach (as described later in the Fair Value Measurement Approaches section) can be used. Whatever method is used should include a risk premium that market participants would likely demand in order to compensate them for the uncertain cash flows of the asset. It may be appropriate to use multiple valuation techniques, and settle upon a point within the range of resulting outcomes that is most representative of fair value.

Identifying Transactions That Are Not Orderly

We noted earlier that fair value is the estimated price at which an asset can be sold or a liability settled in an *orderly* transaction to a third party under current market conditions. How can we tell if a transaction is not orderly? The following points are evidence of such a situation:

- *Inadequate marketing.* A transaction may not have involved a sufficient amount of marketing to attract bidders.
- *Single prospective buyer.* All marketing by the seller was targeted at a single buyer.
- *Distressed.* The seller is in a financially distressed condition, and so is forced to sell on a rushed basis in order to obtain cash.
- *Regulatory requirement.* The seller was forced to sell due to regulatory requirements.
- *Outlier.* The price at which a transaction was settled is well outside of the normal range of prices.

If the conclusion is reached that a transaction was not orderly, place little reliance on that price. If there is not sufficient information to determine whether a transaction was orderly, place a lesser weighting on this transaction than the information gleaned from other transactions that are known to have been orderly.

Highest and Best Use

An additional consideration when determining fair value is the concept of *highest and best use*. Under this concept, fair value is determined based on the price at which an asset could theoretically be employed in its highest and best use, rather than the use in which the asset is currently employed. For an intangible asset, possible highest and best use scenarios include being treated as a stand-alone asset, or with an associated intangible asset, or as part of a bundle of both tangible and intangible assets, or as part of an operating business. Within these scenarios, the highest and best use might involve being retained by the current owner in its current use, or being sold to a different owner, either in its current use or in a different use. Licensing might certainly be considered as the highest and best use of an intangible asset, or using it internally *and* licensing it to third parties.

The highest and best use is subject to the following limitations:

- *Legally permissible*. There may be legal restrictions on how an asset may be used, which bar certain alternative uses. For example, it might be illegal to repurpose a broadcasting license to run a radio station that focuses on sports betting.
- *Physically possible*. The highest and best use should be physically possible, given the attributes of the intangible asset. For example, an environmental permit may only be used within certain tightly-constrained specifications.
- *Financially feasible*. The alternative use must incorporate the costs incurred to convert the asset to that use, while still producing investment returns.
- *Maximum profitability*. Within the constraints of the three preceding limitations, the highest and best use is the one that generates the greatest intangible asset value.

EXAMPLE

Creekside Industrial buys a patent for $1,000,000 that would allow the company to build a technologically-advanced lithium-ion battery. However, Creekside simply sits on the patent, thereby preventing any competitors from using the technology. The fair value of the patent should be based on licensing the patent to competitors, since doing so would yield substantially higher profits than not using the patent, as is currently the case.

The highest and best use concept necessitates the use of estimates regarding income projections, which may result in a range of possible outcomes.

> **Tip:** The applicability of the highest and best use concept will depend on the type of intangible asset. Many of these assets are developed for internal use only (such as engineering drawings), so there is no other use for them.

The Unit of Measure

The fair value of an asset or liability may be in relation to the item as a standalone asset or liability, such as a specific machine or a share of stock. However, it could also refer to a mixed group of assets and liabilities, such as a business that could be sold as a coherent unit. In the latter case, the fair value of the business could be much higher than the sum of its individual assets and liabilities, though it is unlikely to be lower – the business could be broken up and sold as separate assets and liabilities at their individual fair values.

Entry and Exit Prices

When an entity acquires an asset or assumes a liability, the price required to do so is called the *entry price*. After a period of time during which the asset or liability is held, the entity may then sell the asset or pay a third party to take on the liability. In this latter case, the price paid is called the *exit price*. It is possible that there may be a substantial difference between the entry and exit prices.

The exit price may be at some point in the future, and so can only be estimated. The fair value concept drives the entity holding these assets to derive exit prices (not entry prices) based on fair value, even if there is no intent to sell the assets.

When the Transaction Price May Not Equal Fair Value

One might assume that the price at which a transaction is initially recognized is its fair value, but this is not necessarily the case. The entity might have paid or accepted in payment a different amount when any of the following factors are present:

- *Related parties.* The transaction is between related parties, which could mean that there is a strong incentive between the parties to transfer the assets at an unusually high or low price.
- *Duress.* The circumstances might force the seller to accept an unusually low price in exchange for selling an asset. This situation most commonly occurs when a business is approaching bankruptcy, and will enter into unfavorable transactions in order to generate cash. It is also possible that the seller was required to sell in order to meet new regulatory requirements, such as when an acquirer is required by the government to sell off a radio station license as part of an acquisition of another entity.

In these situations, do not place reliance on the information for deriving fair values, for the results could vary significantly from actual fair market values. Conversely, if these factors are not present, *and* the volume of market transactions is large, *and* the comparison transactions are close to the measurement date, the derived fair values can probably be relied upon.

Fair Value Measurement Approaches

There are several general approaches that GAAP permits for deriving fair values. The most favored approaches are those that maximize the use of relevant observable inputs and minimize the use of unobservable inputs. *Observable inputs* are derived from market data that properly reflect the assumptions that third parties would use when setting prices for assets. Examples of markets that are considered to provide observable inputs are dealer markets and brokered markets. The different types of fair value measurement approaches are outlined below:

- *Market approach.* Uses the prices associated with actual market transactions for similar or identical assets to derive a fair value. For example, you could derive a valuation based on market multiples that come from a set of comparable transactions.

- *Income approach.* Uses estimated future cash flows or earnings, adjusted by a discount rate that represents the time value of money and the risk of cash flows not being achieved, to derive a discounted present value. An alternative way to incorporate risk into this approach is to develop a probability-weighted-average set of possible future cash flows.
- *Cost approach.* Uses the estimated cost to replace an asset (or the capabilities of the asset), adjusted for the obsolescence of the existing asset.

None of these measurement approaches is considered to be the preferred method to use. The selection of a method should be based on the availability of information that can be applied to a method and the nature of the item being valued. It can require a detailed knowledge of an asset to determine the best possible method to use.

EXAMPLE

Happy Radio routinely evaluates the fair value of its acquisitions within the broadcasting industry, and so uses the market approach to conduct an annual review of the revenue and EBITDA (earnings before interest, taxes, depreciation and amortization) multiples associated with the broadcasting licenses it has acquired. Accordingly, the acquisitions staff prepares the following multiples analysis.

Name	Market Capitalization	One Year Revenues	One Year EBITDA	Revenue Multiple	EBITDA Multiple
KBRQ Radio	$145,000	$174,000	$19,300	1.2x	7.5x
KCCO Radio	90,000	117,000	11,500	1.3x	7.8x
KDOG Radio	128,000	160,000	24,200	0.8x	5.3x
KGOT Radio	210,000	210,000	30,000	1.0x	7.0x
KMET Radio	52,000	24,000	3,900	2.2x	13.2x
KQUI Radio	360,000	240,000	42,400	1.5x	8.5x
KWAL Radio	76,000	19,000	3,200	4.0x	24.0x
Totals	$1,061,000	$944,000	$134,500	1.1x	7.9x

Thus, the review shows a weighted-average revenue multiple of 1.1x and a weighted-average EBITDA multiple of 7.9x that can be applied to the revenues and EBITDA of its broadcasting licenses to estimate their fair values.

When fair value information can be derived from quotes in an active market, it is probably sufficient to use just one of the preceding methods. However, when inputs are of lesser quality, it may be necessary to employ several methods. In the latter case, there will be a range of possible fair values. If so, a fair value should be selected from this range that is the most representative of fair value, under the specific circumstances involving the entity.

No matter which method is chosen, it may be necessary to include a risk adjustment in the formulation of fair value. This risk adjustment may be a premium that a counterparty would require in order to take on any uncertainties in the cash flows associated with an asset.

Switching Valuation Techniques

Whichever valuation technique is chosen to measure fair value should continue to be used in a consistent manner. However, it is acceptable to alter the technique under certain circumstances if the result is more representative of fair value. Here are several examples of situations in which switching valuation techniques might be warranted:

- *Information is not available.* The entity loses access to information that it formerly used to derive fair values. For example, a database of asset sale prices is taken private and so can no longer be accessed.
- *New information.* The entity gains access to new transaction information that had not been available to it before. For example, a company is acquired and gains access to the parent company's database of asset trading information.
- *New market conditions.* The circumstances of trade in a market may alter, resulting in alterations in the quality of the resulting fair market information. For example, an exchange may limit trading to a smaller group of pre-qualified participants, which reduces the amount of bidding and therefore weakens the quality of the resulting price information.
- *New market.* A new market develops from which better fair value information can be obtained.
- *Valuation methods improve.* The entity may adopt a more sophisticated valuation model. For example, a company's auditors recommend replacing a primitive valuation system with a more refined version that has been forwarded from another client of the auditors.

Hierarchy of Information Sources

The ideal conditions are not always available for obtaining the fair value of an asset or liability. Consequently, GAAP provides a hierarchy of information sources that range from Level 1 (best) to Level 3 (worst). The general intent of these levels of information is to step the accountant through a series of valuation alternatives, where solutions closer to Level 1 are preferred over Level 3. The characteristics of the three levels are as follows:

- *Level 1.* This is a quoted price for an identical item in an active market on the measurement date. This is the most reliable evidence of fair value, and should be used whenever this information is available. It may be necessary to adjust a Level 1 input when a quoted price does not represent fair value, as may be the case when significant events alter the price that parties are willing to pay. When a quoted Level 1 price is adjusted, doing so automatically shifts the result into a lower level. Also, do not alter a Level 1 price just because the company's holdings of a security are quite large in comparison to the normal daily trading volume of the relevant market. Level 1 pricing is commonly available for securities, which may be actively traded in multiple markets, such as the New York Stock Exchange or the NASDAQ.

- *Level 2*. This is directly or indirectly observable inputs other than quoted prices. This definition includes prices for assets or liabilities that are (with key items noted in bold):

  o For **similar** items in active markets; or
  o For identical or similar items in **inactive** markets; or
  o For inputs **other than** quoted prices, such as credit spreads and interest rates; or
  o For inputs **derived from** correlation with observable market data.

  An example of a Level 2 input is a valuation multiple for a business unit that is based on the sale of comparable entities. Another example is the price per square foot for a building, based on prices involving comparable facilities in similar locations.

  It may be necessary to adjust the information derived from Level 2 inputs, since it does not exactly match the assets or liabilities for which fair values are being derived. Adjustments may be needed for such factors as the condition or location of assets and the transaction volume of the markets from which information is derived.

- *Level 3*. This is an unobservable input. It may include the company's own data, adjusted for other reasonably available information. These inputs should reflect the assumptions that would be used by market participants to formulate prices, including assumptions about risk. Examples of a Level 3 input are an internally-generated financial forecast and the prices contained within an offered quote from a distributor.

The information sources in Level 1 are considered to supply the most objective information to the derivation of fair value information, since they are coming from the marketplace. Conversely, the information sources in Level 3 are considered to supply the most subjective information, since they are largely derived internally.

These three levels are known as the *fair value hierarchy*. Please note that these three levels are only used to select inputs to valuation techniques (such as the market approach). The three levels are not used to directly create fair values.

Fair Value Measurement Process Flow

When an organization engages in the measurement of asset fair values, it should obtain the following information:

1. The specific identification of the asset for which a fair value measurement is to be obtained. If the asset is nonfinancial, determine the highest and best use that will be applied to its measurement.
2. The market designated as the principal market for the asset or liability.

3. The valuation technique to be used to develop a fair value.

We have already addressed the concepts of highest and best use and the principal market, which were key components of the preceding fair value process flow. We now turn to one of the valuation techniques that can be used, which is present value analysis. It is based on the discounted cash flows associated with an asset.

Present value is the current worth of cash to be received or spent in the future, which has been discounted at a market rate of interest. The present value of future cash flows is always less than the same amount of future cash flows, since you can immediately invest cash received now, thereby achieving a greater return than from the prospect of cash receipts in the future. The concept is most commonly employed in an electronic spreadsheet. For example, the present value formula in Excel is:

$$(1 \div (1 + \text{Interest rate})^{\wedge} \text{Number of years})$$

As an example, if the discount rate is 10% and you want to determine the discount for cash flows that will occur three years in the future, the Excel calculation is:

$$(1 \div (1 + 0.1)^{\wedge} 3) = 0.75131$$

The easiest way to calculate present value is to use the preceding formula in Excel for the monetary amount and time period in question. However, what if an electronic spreadsheet is not available? The present value discount factor can also be derived from a present value table, which is commonly available in textbooks and on the Internet. The following present value table states the discount factors for the present value of 1 due in N periods for a common range of interest rates.

Present Value Factors for 1 Due in N Periods

Number of Years	6%	7%	8%	9%	10%	11%	12%
1	0.9434	0.9346	0.9259	0.9174	0.9091	0.9009	0.8929
2	0.8900	0.8734	0.8573	0.8417	0.8265	0.8116	0.7972
3	0.8396	0.8163	0.7938	0.7722	0.7513	0.7312	0.7118
4	0.7921	0.7629	0.7350	0.7084	0.6830	0.6587	0.6355
5	0.7473	0.7130	0.6806	0.6499	0.6209	0.5935	0.5674
6	0.7050	0.6663	0.6302	0.5963	0.5645	0.5346	0.5066
7	0.6651	0.6228	0.5835	0.5470	0.5132	0.4817	0.4524
8	0.6274	0.5820	0.5403	0.5019	0.4665	0.4339	0.4039
9	0.5919	0.5439	0.5003	0.4604	0.4241	0.3909	0.3606
10	0.5584	0.5084	0.4632	0.4224	0.3855	0.3522	0.3220
11	0.5268	0.4751	0.4289	0.3875	0.3505	0.3173	0.2875
12	0.4970	0.4440	0.3971	0.3555	0.3186	0.2858	0.2567
13	0.4688	0.4150	0.3677	0.3262	0.2897	0.2575	0.2292
14	0.4423	0.3878	0.3405	0.2993	0.2633	0.2320	0.2046
15	0.4173	0.3625	0.3152	0.2745	0.2394	0.2090	0.1827

To use the table, move to the column representing the relevant interest rate, and move down to the "number of years" row indicating the discount rate to apply to the applicable year of cash flow. Thus, if an analysis were to indicate $100,000 of cash flow in the fourth year, and the interest rate were 10%, multiply the $100,000 by 0.6830 to arrive at a present value of $68,300 for those cash flows.

The interest rate to be used in the present value calculation is the rate on risk-free investments that have durations coinciding with the cash flows being measured. The yield on U.S. Treasury securities is commonly used for this interest rate. This rate should be adjusted to account for the perceived risk of the underlying cash flows. For example, if cash flows were perceived to be highly problematic, a higher discount rate might be justified, which would result in a smaller present value.

An alternative derivation of the discount rate is to use the observed rates of return for comparable assets that are traded in a market. This derivation should only be based on observed rates of return where the nature of the cash flows and other factors are similar to those of the asset being measured. These other factors may include credit scores, the presence of collateral, the duration of cash flows, and the existence of any restrictions on cash flows.

One way to derive fair value with the present value technique is to calculate a probability-weighted average of several possible future cash flows. These are called *expected cash flows*. This approach is most applicable when there are a number of possible cash flow outcomes, and especially when these outcomes are relatively far apart. The following example illustrates the concept, and also employs the use of a risk premium that is applied to the discount rate.

Additional valuation methods will be presented later in this book.

EXAMPLE

There are several possible cash flows expected from the use of an asset. Management assigns the following probabilities to each scenario:

Cash Flow Scenario	Probability	Probability-Weighted Cash Flows
$800,000	10%	$80,000
1,500,000	70%	1,050,000
3,000,000	20%	600,000
	100%	$1,730,000

The risk-free interest rate is 3%, and the estimated risk premium for the variability of cash flows is 4%, for a combined discount rate of 7%. The discounted cash flows of these probability-weighted cash flows are therefore $1,730,000 ÷ 1.07, or $1,616,822. This is the fair value of the asset, using the income approach.

Use of Multiple Valuation Methods

It is allowable to estimate fair value using a number of valuation methods. The result is likely to be a fairly wide range of valuations. If so, it will be necessary to derive a single value from this information that will then be used as the fair value of the asset. The ideal result is one that best represents the asset's fair value. The designation of this fair value point should be the result of a careful evaluation of the inputs to the valuation methods, the nature of the valuation methods, the number of subjective judgments made, and possibly a weighting of the various results. If there is still a wide range of valuations, this can indicate that additional analysis is required.

Ideally, the valuation chosen should maximize the use of observable inputs in the analysis process. Observable inputs are derived from market data that properly reflect the assumptions that third parties would use when setting prices for assets.

EXAMPLE

Mole Industries acquires a company that has developed highly-precise GPS location software Mole intends to incorporate into its ditch digging products. It is not possible to obtain information for a valuation using the market approach, since there are no comparable transactions in the marketplace. The controller can use the income approach to estimate a stream of cash flows, since the company expects that customers will pay a premium if this software is included in their digging machines. This results in a valuation estimate of $2,000,000. The controller also oversees an analysis using the cost approach that estimates what it would cost Mole to develop substitute location software, which indicates a valuation of $1,800,000.

The controller finds that the cost approach valuation of $1,800,000 is questionable, since the acquiree's software used patent-protected technology that would not have been available to someone attempting to reconstruct it. Consequently, he determines that the fair value of the GPS software is $2,000,000, as derived from the income approach.

Summary

A considerable amount of work can be required to devise the fair values of some assets. To lessen the burden, consider avoiding any transactions that will require the company to delve into Level 3 of the fair value hierarchy, where the murky nature of the information requires additional disclosure. Also, try to standardize transactions from period to period, so that the same valuation procedures can be copied forward over time, reducing the amount of original accounting effort that might otherwise be required.

Chapter 3
Valuation Data Gathering

Introduction

When valuing intangible assets, an essential element of the work is data gathering. The documents required for this analysis may relate to historical operations, current operations, and the manner in which the assets may be employed in future operations. These documents are then perused to develop information about how the assets were developed, how they are currently used, and how they could potentially be used in the future. These and other related issues are covered in the following pages.

Indicators for Data Gathering

An early step in the process of data gathering for an asset valuation is to see if there has been a reasonable amount of activity in the marketplace for the sale or licensing of the asset in question. If so, it may be possible to conduct a valuation using the market approach. If there is little evidence of such market interest, then it would probably be wiser to use the income or cost approaches, under the assumption that the asset is only usable internally. These valuation approaches are covered in detail starting in the next chapter.

Data Gathering

When learning about an intangible asset, the main avenues of inquiry are to examine the development of the asset, the operations in which it is used, and how it operates. It is quite possible that little information will initially be available, making the data gathering work especially difficult and time-consuming.

When a valuation is to be derived from the cost approach, it will be especially important to collect information about how the asset was developed. Pertinent questions to address that can assist in setting boundaries around the data collection effort include the following:

- Who was involved in the creation of the asset?
- What were the beginning and ending dates for the asset development effort?
- Are ongoing maintenance expenditures required for the asset to remain usable, such as ongoing lawsuits to protect a trademark or patent? If so, these expenditures should be deducted from any income derivations calculated when using the income method.
- Have additional development efforts been pursued since the asset was initially created? If so, during what date range?
- How is the asset used within the firm's business operations?
- Are other assets needed to ensure that the intangible asset is efficiently used?

- How does the asset provide value to the business? Does it enhance the value of other tangible or intangible assets?
- Could the asset be licensed to a third party?
- Has a third party ever approached the business about acquiring or licensing the asset? If so, at what price?
- Could any events within the industry impact the use of the asset?
- Have there been any prior licensing deals involving the asset? What were their terms?

It may be especially useful to collect the names of those employees who use the asset on a regular basis, since they are the most likely to have more information about it.

Conversely, if the income approach is to be used, then this cost information will be much less relevant. Instead, consider looking for information about the operating income and/or licensing income generated by the asset. Also, consider researching whether it protects the income-generating potential of other company assets. In addition, investigate whether the asset reduces expenses or capital costs in any way. The manager who oversees how the asset is used may be in the best position to assist with the collection of this information.

Tip: Document all economic benefits extensively, tracing them back to the general ledger where possible. Doing so provides evidence in case an auditor wants proof of why a particular asset value was used.

When an intangible asset was recently recognized, a reasonable way to determine its financial impact is by comparing the financial results of the business before it was introduced to its impact afterwards.

Tip: When the value of an intangible asset is based – at least in part – on future financial projections, verify that any corporate bottlenecks will not limit the amount of these projections that can actually be realized.

EXAMPLE

A snow cat operator has obtained a U.S. Forest Service permit to operate 10,000 skier days between the months of December and April in an especially snowy section of national forest. However, the value of this permit is constrained, because the operator only has access to two snow cats, which can only carry 12 clients each per day. This means that the firm can only achieve 3,624 skier days within the specified operating date range.

It is also useful to gather information about how the asset contributes to or protects the competitive position of the business. For example, does it have a direct impact on how well the firm competes in the marketplace? Or, can it be used to defend the organization's income sources or assets? This investigation can also address the extent to which the asset could be infringed upon by a competitor, and how well it is being protected through the use of noncompetition agreements, nondisclosure agreements, and so forth.

A further line of inquiry is to investigate whether competitors have a comparable asset. If so, see if there is any industry information about how these competing assets were built or purchased. This could lead to an investigation into the likely cost of these assets. This investigation could be expanded to see if there is a common useful life for this type of asset, which could indicate the period over which income or cash flows from it could be expected.

> **Tip:** If a competitor has been purchased recently, see if the acquirer reported the fair value of the targeted intangible asset(s) in its financial statements. This will only be possible if the acquirer is publicly-held.

> **Tip:** See if there is a commonly-used valuation benchmark within the industry for the asset in question, such as a price per customer for a customer list, or a price per subscriber for a subscriber list.

Yet another line of inquiry is whether pending regulatory changes will alter the value of the asset (such as on an existing broadcast license when the FCC is considering issuing additional licenses into the same market). If such changes are looming, they could seriously alter the expected future benefits to be derived from an intangible asset.

Additional Considerations

There are other considerations to keep in mind when engaged in the data gathering process. One issue is certainly that the valuation of an intangible asset is somewhat dependent on the economic conditions prevailing as of the valuation date. Since economic conditions are constantly in a state of flux, you should only take subsequent conditions into account to the extent that they could have been predicted at the valuation date; all other subsequent conditions should be ignored.

Summary

This chapter has only provided general indicators of where to search for data that could be used in the valuation of an intangible asset. The problem is that many businesses do not keep detailed information about these assets, which may call for innovative approaches to how a valuation might be achieved.

Chapter 4
Cost Approach Valuation

Introduction

Under a cost approach valuation, the analyst is trying to devise a value for an intangible asset based on what it would cost to create it from scratch. This approach is based on the premise that a prudent third-party purchaser would pay no more for an asset than its replacement cost. This approach is most commonly used when an asset does not directly generate income, in which case the income approach to valuation is not possible. It is also used when there is no ready market for the sale of the asset, which eliminates the market approach to valuation as an option. In this chapter, we cover the issues to be aware of when developing a cost approach valuation.

When to Use the Cost Approach

Using the cost approach is most applicable when the intangible asset is relatively new, and could be exchanged for another similar asset. For example, software developed in-house using one programming language could be exchanged for software developed elsewhere using a different programming language, but which has approximately the same functionality.

The cost approach is also more applicable when the owner intends to keep using the intangible asset on an ongoing basis. This is because, in the absence of the asset, the owner would have to create a substitute for the asset or obtain the use of an asset owned by someone else, in exchange for a royalty payment.

Conversely, the cost approach should not be used to value older intangible assets. It should also not be used for intellectual property, since the special legal protections afforded to such property can be especially hard to value. For example, it would be extremely difficult to calculate a cost to replicate a famous brand name. Also, it is impossible to devise the cost of something that has trademark or copyright protection, since these legal protections would keep anyone from replacing the intangible asset in question.

Defining the Asset

In many cases, it is simple enough to define what the asset is that will be valued – it is a single broadcast license, or computer program, for example. However, sometimes the definition is less clear, such as when a company wants to value an entire computer system, which may be comprised of dozens of internally-generated computer programs. In the latter situation, you should spend time up front, carefully defining the assets to be valued. Otherwise, a poor definition may result in a seriously incorrect valuation.

Defining the asset can involve the collection of information about the number of intangible assets to be valued, how each one is described, how long ago it was developed or obtained, the amount of its original cost, and when the owner expects to retire it. The analyst should also verify the accuracy of this information and the existence of the associated asset to the greatest extent possible. This information provides an adequate starting point for a cost approach valuation.

Costs to Use in the Cost Approach

There are two types of cost that can be used in a cost approach valuation. One approach is to use *reproduction cost new*, which is the cost that would be incurred to create a duplicate of the asset as of the analysis date. Under this approach, you would assume that all of the flaws and unusual benefits of the existing asset would be incorporated into the reproduced asset, as well as its current level of obsolescence. Alternatively, you could develop a cost based on *replacement cost new*, which is the cost that would be incurred to create an asset with the same utility level of the current asset – but using the most modern approach to the development work, and without the inclusion of any flaws or unusual benefits of the existing asset, or any consideration of obsolescence.

The replacement cost new approach can result in a lower cost than the reproduction cost new, since the replacement approach uses the latest (and presumably most efficient) development methods. Nonetheless, the two outcomes tend to result in quite similar cost outcomes. That being the case, you should pick whichever method has the greatest quantity of high-grade costing information available.

Note: When using the cost approach, it is generally assumed that the original intellectual content is already known, so that the content does not have to be re-invented. If this is not the case, then the cost may be substantially higher.

No matter which approach is used, the cost components to be applied to the analysis will be the same. They are the direct costs, indirect costs, developer's profit, and entrepreneurial incentive, and are explained as follows:

- *Direct costs*. These are the costs of labor, materials, and overhead directly incurred by the creator of the asset. Examples of labor costs are programmer salaries and contractor payments; they may comprise the largest part of direct costs. Examples of material costs are computer equipment, audio tape masters, and drawing supplies; they tend to be quite a small part of the development of intangible assets. Examples of overhead are payroll taxes, fringe benefits, and supervisory costs.
- *Indirect costs*. These are the costs of labor, materials, and overhead indirectly incurred by the creator of the asset. Examples of these costs are law firm fees, testing laboratory fees, and marketing study costs.
- *Developer's profit*. This is the return the developer expects on funds invested in the development process. It may be calculated as a percentage mark-up, or as a percentage return on direct and indirect costs.

- *Entrepreneurial incentive*. This is the opportunity cost of the creator of the intangible asset. In essence, it is the economic benefit needed to persuade the asset creator to develop the asset. The foregone cash flow during the development period could be considered the creator's opportunity cost. It may also be considered compensation for the risk of failure that the creator undertakes during the asset development process.

Consideration of Obsolescence

The preceding derivation of cost should also include a deduction for obsolescence, on the grounds that the asset being valued is usually not new; instead, it may have been in existence for a number of years, and may not even have much time left in its estimated useful life.

It is especially important to consider obsolescence when the cost approach is used, since this estimation approach derives costs as though the asset were new. This replacement asset would likely be superior to the actual intangible asset in some respects, so its value must be adjusted downward to account for this difference.

> **Note:** The consideration of obsolescence is not necessary when the intangible asset in question is also new.

There are several types of obsolescence that can apply to an intangible asset. One is *functional obsolescence*, where the asset can no longer perform the function(s) for which it was originally intended. This is a common issue with some types of intangible assets. For example, software that was originally designed to monitor an in-house production process might not work so well over time, as the underlying production process changes. Or, a patent is worth less over time, as other innovations arise that render it less useful. An indicator of functional obsolescence is when it would cost less to create an intangible asset today than it actually did. Another indicator of functional obsolescence is when the cost to maintain an asset has been increasing over time. The present value of this trend line in excess operating costs into the future can be used to quantify functional obsolescence.

EXAMPLE

Grunge Motor Sports recognized the value of the assembled workforce when it acquired a competitor. However, due to the imposition of a variety of automation improvements in the acquiree's production lines, it now has more employees on staff than it really needs. Since these excess employees are not adding value to the assembled workforce asset, the analyst could consider adjusting the replacement cost of this asset in a downward direction.

Another type of obsolescence is *external obsolescence*. This is a decline in the value of an intangible asset, which is caused by external events, and which are usually outside of the owner's control. For example, the passage of a law to cut back on the number of broadcast licenses could result in the removal of a license authorization, thereby rendering it obsolete.

Functional and external obsolescence can be subtracted from the calculated reproduction cost new of an intangible asset to arrive at its replacement cost new. The formula is as follows:

Reproduction cost new – Functional obsolescence – External obsolescence
= Replacement cost new

A further consideration is whether an identified form of obsolescence is curable or incurable. It is curable when the benefit associated with enhancing the asset exceeds the cost of doing so. It is incurable when this benefit is less than the cost of enhancing the asset. This concept only applies to functional obsolescence, since external obsolescence is usually considered to be beyond the control of the asset owner.

One way to determine obsolescence is to estimate the total useful life of an asset, and then calculate the to-date amount of obsolescence, based on the number of years that have already passed. For example, if an asset is considered to have a total useful life of eight years and two of those years have already passed, then the asset can be considered 25% obsolete.

Variations on the Concept

A variation on the cost approach is to measure the costs that are being avoided because the owner possesses the intangible asset. These costs are avoided because the owner does not have to pay a royalty for the use of a comparable asset owned by someone else.

Case Study

Horton Corporation has purchased Hubble Corporation, and wants to derive the value of its satellite tracking software, which was developed internally. This value will then be recognized as part of the accounting for the acquisition. The analyst tasked with this activity accesses Hubble's project records to determine the amount of the software developer hours consumed to create the software. This amount was 3,500 hours, at an average compensation rate of $60 per hour, for a total of $210,000. In addition, the analyst determines the amount of administrative overhead for other staff who worked on the project, which totaled $42,000. This is also a direct cost of the project, as is the $68,000 of benefits and payroll taxes paid to the people involved in the work. Thus, the actual direct costs of the asset, as per Hubble's records, total $320,000.

The analyst then conducts an analysis to determine how much it would cost to reconstruct the software, using Hubble's procedures for designing and testing software. This is the replacement cost new approach. She brings in a software consultant to advise on the number of hours required to develop the various modules of the software, assuming a standard contractor rate of $90 per hour. This analysis concludes that 3,000 hours would be required, which comes to a cost of $270,000.

The analyst cannot find any indirect costs that could be applied to a replacement cost new analysis.

In addition, the analyst concludes that a 15% developer's profit would be required to attract the team required to conduct the work, based on an analysis of what several developer firms in the area charge for similar types of work. This profit represents an additional cost of $40,500. Without the developer's profit, it would be impossible to attract a qualified development firm.

The analyst also examines the entrepreneurial incentive cost component. This is needed to incentivize the owner to develop the software, rather than using the required funds for some other investment project. One way to do so is to calculate a fair rate of return on the total cost components of the intangible asset, on the grounds that the owner would not develop the asset in the absence of an adequate rate of return. The company's cost of capital is 12%, which is applied to the total investment of $310,500. Since the presumed development period is six months, the rate of return on the invested funds for this period would be $18,630.

In short, the replacement cost new of the software would be as follows:

Direct costs	$270,000
Developer's profit	40,500
Entrepreneurial incentive	18,630
Total replacement cost new	$329,130

The analyst must also consider the obsolescence of the software. She learns from Hubble's senior satellite tracking team that about a fifth of the functionality of the software will shortly become obsolete, when the company gains access to NASA software that performs the same function. The remainder of the software should be usable for the foreseeable future. This functional obsolescence represents a 20% reduction in the replacement cost new of the asset, which reduces its value to $263,304. This figure represents the amount that a willing buyer would pay for the satellite tracking software, and is more than $56,000 lower than a compilation of the actual costs incurred by the business to originally create the software.

Summary

The calculated cost of an intangible asset does not necessarily equate to its value. Nonetheless, the calculated cost should provide a reasonably close approximation of value when all cost components have been included in the derivation, as well as all forms of obsolescence that may apply to it. It is especially useful when there is no income directly associated with the asset (which eliminates the use of an income approach valuation).

Chapter 5
Market Approach Valuation

Introduction

The market approach to valuation is used when there are records of sales or licensing agreements for similar intangible assets between other parties. Since these are market transactions, they can provide convincing evidence of the value of a comparable asset. In this chapter, we cover the types of market valuations, normalization adjustments, and several related issues.

When to Use the Market Approach

The market approach is warranted whenever there is an active market for the sale of similar intangible assets. Examples of these assets are broadcast licenses, trademarks, and franchises. This approach is especially relevant when similar sales or licensing transactions have occurred recently, and especially in volume. When there is a rich source of data on which to base valuation decisions, it is much easier to develop a defensible valuation.

Conversely, it may not be possible to use the market approach when the nature of the other transactions in the marketplace differs significantly from the asset you are attempting to value. For example, the licensor of an asset might be willing to provide legal protection for it, as well as supportive advertising – for which the value must be stripped out for your valuation purposes. In this case, the adjustment from market data may be so large as to make the valuation highly suspect. Or, the market data involves the sale of a bundle of assets, from which it may not be possible to separate out the value of a single asset.

Normalization Adjustments

There are several ways in which an ostensibly comparable market transaction might contain elements that differ from the characteristics of the asset you are trying to value. Here are several elements of the comparison in which there may be differences:

- How the asset can be used under the terms of the agreement
- The duration of the transaction
- The economic conditions impacting the transaction
- The financing terms associated with the transaction
- The nature of the ownership rights being licensed or sold
- Whether other assets were included in the transaction
- Whether the transaction was conducted in an arm's-length manner

When using market data to derive a market-based asset valuation, it may be necessary to normalize the data to make it more applicable to the valuation of the asset in question. Here are several types of adjustments that may need to be made:

- Adjust for subsequent changes in asset pricing, if the comparison transaction was not recent.
- Strip out the impact of additional sale features in the comparison transaction, such as the licensor providing legal protection for a license.
- Adjust for unusual financing features in the comparison transaction, such as an unusually high interest rate charged to a licensee.
- Adjust for unusually high demand in the comparison transaction, such as when a licensee needs to acquire a license to take advantage of a short-term window of opportunity in the market.
- Adjust for an unusually low price on the comparison transaction, if the licensor accepted a low price because it was in immediate need of cash.

Setting a Pricing Metric

There are many ways to set up a pricing metric for use in creating a market-based valuation. The basic approach is to divide the price of a market transaction by a financial or operational variable. The exact approach used will depend on the nature of the intangible asset. Here are several possible pricing metrics that could be used:

- Price as a multiple of book value
- Price per customer
- Price per dollar of revenue or profit generated
- Price per drawing
- Price per expected customers gained
- Price per future revenue or profit dollar
- Price per line of software code
- Price per potential customer or patient
- Price per subscriber
- Price per unit manufactured
- Price per use

Types of Market Valuations

When valuing an intangible asset under the market approach, any of the following three approaches may be used:

- The sales of similar assets in arm's-length transactions, or the rates at which comparable assets are being licensed to third parties. More recent transaction data will be more relevant to the valuation.
- A comparison of the profit margin being earned by the business with the intangible asset to other similar organizations that do not own a similar asset.

- The relief from royalty method, which is based on the royalty rate that the organization would otherwise have to pay a third party to use a similar intangible asset.

We address each of these types of valuations in the following sub-sections.

Sales Comparison Method

The sales comparison method should only be used when there is an ongoing history of similar assets being separately sold in the marketplace, as is the case with (for example) credit card portfolios and mortgage servicing rights. Information about these transactions can be found in public company filings, company press releases, trade journals, news articles, academic publications, and so forth.

> **Note:** The sales comparison method should not be used when the comparable transactions involve complex pricing, including such features as earnouts and contingency payments. It is too difficult to convert these transactions into a price per unit.

Once comparable transactions have been found, the prices paid must be converted into a price per unit (see the earlier Setting a Pricing Metric section), such as $10 per customer or $20 per line of software code. This analysis is conducted for all of the comparable transactions, resulting in a statistical analysis that shows the range of prices, price quartiles, price mean, and so forth. This information can then be applied to the derivation of a valuation for the asset in question.

Comparable Profit Margin Method

The comparable profit margin method involves comparing the profit margins being earned by a business with an intangible asset to similar entities that do not own such an asset. This approach has limited applicability, since it is most useful only when the asset in question is an exceptional one that greatly contributes to the profitability of the business (such as a manufacturing process or trade secret), and when competitors do not possess anything like it. If this situation is present, then the comparison companies usually need to be within the same industry.

Conversely, the comparable profit margin method should not be used when the owner has a large number of intangible assets, none of which individually contribute a large amount to profits. This approach should also not be used when the comparison firms are supported by their own exceptional intangible assets that give them unusually high profit levels.

When using this method, the essential activities are to locate comparison companies, then calculate the net profits of these parties, and then compare their margins to those of the owner business. Finally, the excess profits generated by the owner business over those of the comparison group are used to derive the value of the intangible asset. The derivation involves setting up a table, in which is listed the expected excess future income of the owner business, which is then reduced to its present value through the application of a discount rate. This present value is the value of the intangible asset.

When conducting the analysis, the net profits of the comparison parties are calculated as the percentage of earnings before interest and taxes (EBIT). Using EBIT allows you to eliminate from the analysis any variations in financing costs and taxes in the other businesses, leaving just operating earnings.

EXAMPLE

Cuppy Corporation owns a secret manufacturing process that can create foam cups at an exceptionally low cost and minimal scrap levels. Its EBIT profit percentage has averaged 25% for the past three years, while the EBIT for a comparison group has been 15% during that period. The 10% excess margin experienced by Cuppy resulted in an average of $200,000 excess EBIT in the past year. This information is reflected in the following table, where the company assumes a 3% annual growth rate in excess EBIT. The 10% discount rate reflects the company's cost of capital. The outcome is a fair value estimate of $632,413 for the manufacturing process.

	Year 1	Year 2	Year 3	Year 4	Year 5
Expected excess EBIT	$200,000	$206,000	$212,180	$218,545	$225,102
Income taxes @ 21%	-42,000	-43,260	-44,559	-45,894	-47,271
After-tax excess EBIT	158,000	162,740	167,621	172,651	177,831
Present value factor	.9091	.8265	.7513	.6830	.6209
Present value	$143,638	$134,505	$125,934	$117,921	$110,415

Relief from Royalty Method

The relief from royalty method is based on the royalty rate that a firm would otherwise have to pay a third party to use a similar intangible asset. It should be used when the intent of the analysis is to derive the appropriate royalty rate. This means that the method is most commonly used for intangible assets that are routinely licensed, such as proprietary technology, trademarks, and franchises.

Once comparable assets have been found on which royalty rates are charged, the selected royalty rate (or range of rates) is multiplied by the company's revenue that relates to the asset. The outcome is a royalty expense that the owner does not have to pay, since it already owns the asset. The amount of this royalty expense avoided can then be capitalized to arrive at the value of the underlying asset.

Note: The royalty expense may also be derived by multiplying the selected royalty rate by the related number of units produced, related profit, or some similar measure.

EXAMPLE

Quest Clothiers has just acquired Himalayan Express, a purveyor of adventure-ready business wear. Quest's accountants want to assign a value to the Himalayan Express trademark. Other clothing companies routinely license their trademarks, so there is a market from which royalty rate information can be obtained. An analysis of royalty rates for adjacent brands within the past year reveals that a 5% royalty rate would be applicable.

The value of the Himalayan Express trademark is the present value of the expected savings (after-tax) from the 5% royalty rate. This calculation appears in the following table, where the company assumes a 4% annual growth rate in the company's revenue from the Himalayan Express product line for the next five years. The 12% discount rate reflects the company's cost of capital. The outcome is a fair value estimate of $3,058,000 for the trademark.

(000s)	Year 1	Year 2	Year 3	Year 4	Year 5
Expected revenue	$20,000	$20,800	$21,632	$22,497	$23,397
License royalty rate	5%	5%	5%	5%	5%
Pre-tax royalty relief	1,000	1,040	1,082	1,125	1,170
Income taxes @ 21%	-210	-218	-227	-236	-246
After-tax royalty relief	790	822	855	889	924
Present value factor	.8929	.7972	.7118	.6355	.5674
Present value	$705	$655	$609	$565	$524

Summary

The market approach can be an exceedingly useful way to derive the valuation of an intangible asset, but only when there is a significant amount of data for similar transactions that have been occurring recently in the marketplace. If this is not the case, then the income approach – as described in the next chapter – might be a good alternative.

Chapter 6
Income Approach Valuation

Introduction

When there is a consistent stream of income associated with an intangible asset, then a good valuation alternative is the income approach. This option works best when the income can be directly associated with a specific asset. If not, then one of the other valuation approaches described in the previous chapters might be a better alternative. In this chapter, we describe the components of the income approach and provide several examples of its use.

When to Use the Income Approach

The income approach can be used whenever an intangible asset produces either operating income or licensing income. This income can be generated either through the direct use of the asset (such as a license to operate a nuclear power plant), or by licensing it, or through defensive use where it is denied to other parties (such as with a patent or copyright). Further, it can be applied to groups of intangible assets, not just individual ones. For example, several hundred franchise agreements could be bundled together for an income-based valuation.

> **Tip:** It can make sense to disaggregate a bundle of intangible assets for valuation purposes when they have differing revenue growth rates or profit margins. This should result in several smaller bundles of assets whose characteristics are more similar to each other.

Components of the Income Approach

When devising an asset valuation based on the income approach, you must estimate three components of the calculation, which are described in the following sub-sections.

Income Estimation

Income may be calculated for an intangible asset that directly produces operating income. For example, an assembled workforce asset can generate income, as can a manufacturing process. A common alternative is to generate income indirectly, through licensing. This can involve a flat fee being paid by the licensee, a percentage of revenue, a profit split, a guaranteed minimum payment, a fee per unit produced, or some variation (or combination) of these concepts.

A less-common use of an asset is to block the activities of a competitor. For example, obtaining a patent on a product design keeps competitors from offering that specific design. In essence, the example represents the defensive nonuse of the patent to protect the market position of the patent holder. As another example, a business might obtain a patent on a next-generation widget, but elects not to use it so that the company can continue to earn profits from its prior generation of the widget. In this case, the income generated is the amount that would be lost if the asset owner were to commercialize the patent.

When estimating the income for an intangible asset, you may apply the highest and best use of the asset, which could be any of the preceding forms of income generation, and not necessarily how it is currently being used.

There are several ways to estimate income, as noted in the following bullet points:

- *Associate incremental income gains with the asset.* The owner of the asset enjoys an incremental boost to its revenues or an incremental decline in its costs by owning the asset. This could be caused by adding new products or customers, increased prices, or reduced product returns. Or, cost reductions could be achieved by shrinking research, production, or selling expenses. There may also be a cost reduction because the owner can now invest in fewer assets. The asset might even reduce the risk level of the business, which reduces its cost of capital. The more common ways to devise incremental income are as follows:

  o Decreased investment
  o Enhanced production efficiency
  o Extended time period over which revenue can be generated
  o Increased demand for related products
  o Increased market share
  o Increased number of customers
  o Increased price point
  o Increased revenue
  o Reduced cost of goods sold
  o Reduced equipment maintenance costs
  o Reduced freight costs
  o Reduced labor costs
  o Reduced product returns
  o Reduced production scrap
  o Reduced promotional costs

- *Calculate income with and without the asset.* When it is not possible to directly measure the income generated by an asset, compare the owner's actual income to a benchmark measure, such as the industry's average profitability level.
- *Calculate residual income for the asset.* In this more complicated approach, you identify all owner assets that contribute to the generation of income (such as working capital, real estate, and fixed assets), and assign a reasonable rate of return to each one. All remaining income after these returns are subtracted is the residual income associated with the intangible asset. This analysis could

be based on cash flow, rather than profits. This approach is typically only used when a business only reports income for the entire entity, and has no way of tracking it by individual asset.

- *Link relief from royalty to the asset.* The owner can calculate the amount of royalty that would have to be paid for the asset if it did not own it. This rate is based on what other asset owners are charging for licensing agreements for similar assets. See the Market Approach Valuation chapter for more information.

No matter which of these methods is used, you may also need to consider whether the costs to maintain the intangible asset will change over time. If so, this can impact the amount of income received in each estimation period.

Another consideration is whether to employ sensitivity analysis, to see if there are any variables that could significantly alter the expected level of income associated with an asset. This analysis can provide insights into scenarios that might have material impacts on the valuation. This may result in the assignment of probabilities to each scenario, resulting in a median value being used as the asset valuation.

Income Duration

The time period over which income is expected to be received in relation to the intangible asset is a key part of the income valuation calculation. Most intangible assets do not have a presumed unlimited life, so some cap must be placed on the number of years over which related income is assumed to be received.

Tip: If the income generated from an intangible asset is expected to vary a great deal over time, then it might be necessary to adopt a quarterly or even a monthly measurement interval. For most assets, an annual measurement interval is the most common usage.

For valuation purposes, the assumed period of time over which income will be received is usually the shortest one over which income can be reasonably expected. For example, if a patent has 10 years left to run, but will be technologically superseded in two years, then the duration of income from it should be limited to just the next two years.

In cases where a patent is set to expire soon, it may be possible to extend the presumed income from it for a modest additional period of time, on the assumption that it will take time for competitors to incorporate the knowledge represented by the patent into their own product offerings and processes. If so, it may be necessary to assume declining income over the extended period, as more and more competitors take advantage of the expired patent.

Income Approach Valuation

Income Capitalization Rate

A capitalization rate is needed to convert the income associated with an income stream to an asset valuation. There are two ways to arrive at a capitalization rate. One is to develop a present value discount rate, which applies a discount rate to the expected income stream to arrive at a present value for the asset. This approach works best when income is expected to vary over time. The other option is to develop a direct capitalization rate, which can be used when there is an expectation of consistent income over an extended period of time (in essence, an annuity), so that a single annuity present value discount rate can be applied to the expected income for all periods.

In either case, the capitalization rate should be forward-looking, incorporating the owner's risk in being able to achieve the expected income level. For example, a risk-free capitalization rate might be 10%, while an asset for which the related income stream might be quite difficult to achieve could warrant a much higher rate, such as 18%. A higher capitalization rate will result in a lower present value, and therefore a lower valuation for an asset.

EXAMPLE

Creekside Industrial acquires a competitor, Advanced Ampere. Both companies manufacture batteries. Ampere has a substantial list of customers, for which Creekside wants to develop a value for its customer relationships intangible asset. There is a relatively high degree of customer turnover in the industry, so Creekside elects to limit the income estimation period to just three years. Its valuation analysis appears in the following table, which summarizes the income likely to be generated from its existing customer base over the next three years. There is an assumed 20% annual decline in these revenues over the three-year period, to reflect the assumed loss of customers. The present value discount rate is set at 10%.

(000s)	Year 1	Year 2	Year 3
Sales	$20,000	$16,000	$12,800
- Cost of sales	12,000	9,600	7,680
- Operating expenses	6,000	5,000	4,000
= Pre-tax profit	2,000	1,400	1,120
- Income tax expense (21%)	420	294	235
= After-tax profit	1,580	1,106	885
+ Depreciation	500	450	400
- Capital expenditures	100	100	100
+ Working capital decline	--	250	250
= Intangible asset income	2,180	1,706	1,435
Present value discount	.9091	.8265	.7513
Present value of intangible asset	$1,982	$1,410	$1,078

The result is a valuation of $4,470,000 for the customer relationships intangible asset, which Creekside records as part of its acquisition accounting for the purchase of Advanced Ampere.

35

EXAMPLE

Pianoforte International manufactures a variety of pianos. It has developed an automated piano production line that allows it to eliminate 90% of the labor costs from its production processes. The company's owners are considering selling the business, and want to put a value on the intellectual property associated with this production line. To do so, the company controller decides to use the residual income approach to derive the value of this asset. She starts by adjusting every line item on the company's balance sheet to its current fair market value, which appears in the following table. The table does not include any equity line items, which are irrelevant to the analysis.

	Book Value	Value Adjustments	Fair Value
Cash	$300,000	--	$300,000
Accounts receivable	2,000,000	--	2,000,000
Inventory	800,000	-100,000	700,000
Fixed assets	5,000,000	-300,000	4,700,000
Total assets	$8,100,000	-$400,000	$7,700,000
Accounts payable	600,000	--	600,000
Accrued expenses	100,000	--	100,000
Long-term debt	2,000,000	--	2,000,000
Other liabilities	400,000	--	400,000
Total liabilities	$3,100,000	$--	$3,100,000

Of these amounts, the assets that contribute to the generation of operating income are working capital (with a fair value of $2,100,000) and fixed assets (with a fair value of $4,700,000).

The total income generated by Pianoforte in its most recent year of operations was $1,000,000. The controller estimates that a fair rate of return on its assets is 12%. This works out to a return on identified assets of $816,000 (calculated as $6,800,000 of identified assets × 12%). The difference between the $1,000,000 of income and the return on identified assets is $184,000, which is assigned to the intellectual property asset.

The controller elects to capitalize this income on the assumption that the intangible asset will continue to generate the same income over the next five years. The discount rate for a five-year annuity using the firm's 10% cost of capital is 3.7908, which results in a capitalized value for the asset of $697,507 (calculated as $184,000 of income × 3.7908 discount rate for the present value of an ordinary annuity of 1).

Summary

The income approach works well for the valuation of many types of intangible assets, as long as income can be directly associated with them. It requires a detailed analysis of the income associated with a specific asset, which makes its valuation outcomes highly defensible. However, it is also possible to alter a valuation through excessively generous (or parsimonious) income, expense, or capitalization rate assumptions. Consequently, extensive documentation of all assumptions is highly recommended, along with a detailed supervisory verification of these numbers.

Chapter 7
Internally-Generated Intangible Assets

Introduction

As a general rule, internally-generated intangible assets are not recognized as assets on an organization's books. Instead, they are charged to expense as incurred. Much of the preceding discussion has centered on the valuation of intangible assets that have been acquired as part of a business combination or purchased from a third party – which are the main situations in which the value of intangible assets *can* be recognized. We clarify when internally-generated intangible assets can be recognized as assets in the following pages.

Acquired Intangible Assets

Though we have just pointed out that the main point of this chapter is internally-generated intangible assets, we will digress for a moment to describe the treatment of acquired intangible assets. When an intangible asset is acquired, the amount of consideration paid for it is recorded as the recognized cost of the asset. This includes any related transaction costs. If a non-cash form of consideration is paid for the asset, then the fair value of either the asset paid or the asset received is used as the recognized cost of the intangible asset – whichever one is more reliably measurable.

Internal-Use Software

Companies routinely develop software for internal use, and want to understand how these development costs are to be accounted for. Software is considered to be for internal use when it has been acquired or developed *only* for the internal needs of a business. Examples of situations where software is considered to be developed for internal use are:

- Accounting systems
- Cash management tracking systems
- Customer service software
- Data collection and analysis systems
- Database search tools
- Membership tracking systems
- Production automation systems
- Video production systems

Further, there can be no reasonably possible plan to market the software outside of the company, as would be the case when a marketing channel has been selected that has specifically-identified promotional, delivery, billing, and support activities. A market feasibility study is not considered a reasonably possible marketing plan, nor is an arrangement that provides for the joint development of software for mutual internal use. However, a history of selling software that had initially been developed for internal use creates a reasonable assumption that the latest internal-use product will also be marketed for sale outside of the company.

EXAMPLE

Harrison Manufacturing develops just-in-time software that it uses internally to monitor the flow of jobs through its production process. The IT manager convinces management to sell the JIT software outside the company, which meets with some success. Subsequently, the firm develops warehouse management software to manage the flow of goods through its own distribution warehouses. Since Harrison has a history of selling its internally-developed software outside of the firm, there is a reasonable assumption that the same action will be taken for the new warehouse management software – which prevents the firm from accounting for it as internal-use software. Instead, it must account for the new software using the requirements for software that is intended for sale.

EXAMPLE

Inouye Semiconductor uses highly-complex wafer testing software to determine whether the semiconductor chips it is producing are operational. This is internal-use software, since customers do not acquire the software, nor do they obtain the future right to use it.

The accounting for internal-use software varies, depending upon the stage of completion of the project. The relevant accounting is:

- *Stage 1: Preliminary project activities.* All costs incurred during the preliminary stage of a development project should be charged to expense as incurred. This stage is considered to include making decisions about the allocation of resources, determining performance requirements, conducting supplier demonstrations, evaluating technology, and supplier selection.
- *Stage 2: Application development.* Capitalize the costs incurred to develop internal-use software, which may include coding, hardware installation, and testing. Any costs related to data conversion, user training, administration, and overhead should be charged to expense as incurred. Data conversion may include purging or cleansing existing data, reconciling old and new data, and converting old data to the new system. Only the following costs can be capitalized:
  o Materials and services consumed in the development effort, such as third-party development fees, software purchase costs, and travel costs related to development work.
  o Costs to develop or acquire software that allow for access to or conversion of old data by new systems.

- o The payroll and benefit costs of those employees directly associated with software development, to the extent of the time spent directly on the project.
- o The capitalization of interest costs incurred to fund the project. These costs can only be capitalized for the period during which there are activities related to software development.

- *Stage 3. Post-implementation.* Charge all post-implementation costs to expense as incurred. Examples of these costs are training and maintenance costs.

Any allowable capitalization of costs should begin *after* the preliminary stage has been completed, management authorizes and commits to funding the project, it is probable that the project will be completed, and the software will be used for its intended function.

The capitalization of costs should end when all substantial testing has been completed. If it is no longer probable that a project will be completed, stop capitalizing the costs associated with it, and conduct impairment testing on the costs already capitalized. The cost at which the asset should then be carried is the lower of its carrying amount or fair value (less costs to sell). Unless there is evidence to the contrary, the usual assumption is that uncompleted software has no fair value. The following are general indicators that software is no longer expected to be completed and placed in service:

- Expenditures are no longer being budgeted or incurred for the software.
- There are programming difficulties that will not be resolved on a timely basis.
- There have been significant cost overruns.
- The costs that have been or will be incurred significantly exceed the cost of competing third-party software, so management intends to stop development and buy the third-party software.
- New technology in the marketplace is driving management to acquire third-party products, rather than completing the internal development project.
- The business unit to which the software relates is either unprofitable or will be discontinued.

Any later upgrades of the software can be capitalized, but only if it is probable that extra system functionality will result from the upgrade. These upgrades typically require the formulation of new software specifications, which may alter some portion of the existing specifications. The costs of maintaining the system should be charged to expense as incurred.

The capitalized cost of internal-use software should be routinely reviewed for impairment. The following are all indicators of the possible presence of asset impairment:

- The software is not expected to be of substantive use
- The manner in which the software was originally intended to be used has now changed

- The software is to be significantly altered
- The development cost of the software significantly exceeded original expectations

Once a business has developed software for internal use, management may decide to market it for external use by third parties. If so, the proceeds from software licensing, net of selling costs, should be applied against the carrying amount of the software asset. For the purposes of this topic, selling costs are considered to include commissions, software reproduction costs, servicing obligations, warranty costs, and installation costs. The business should not recognize a profit on sales of the software until the application of net sales to the carrying amount of the software asset have reduced the carrying amount to zero. The business can recognize all further proceeds as revenue.

Internal-Use Software Accessed via a Hosting Arrangement

The preceding guidance also applies to internal-use software to which the organization gains access via a hosting arrangement – but only if both of the following criteria are met:

- The company has the contractual right to take possession of the software at any time without incurring a significant penalty; and
- It is feasible to run the software on the company's own hardware, or contract with a third party to host the software.

When the preceding criteria are not met, then the hosting arrangement is considered to be a service contract, and so does not constitute a software purchase.

Under a hosting arrangement, it is relatively common for the price to include several elements, such as the software license, hosting, and employee training. When this is the case, the company should allocate the price paid among these various elements, where the allocation is based on the standalone price of each element in the contract.

The accountant should examine the capitalized costs associated with a hosting arrangement for impairment when any of the following conditions are present:

- The arrangement is not expected to provide any substantive service potential to the company.
- A significant change has occurred in the extent to which the hosting arrangement is used.
- A significant change has been made to the hosting arrangement.

Website Development Costs

A company may allocate funds to the development of a company website in such areas as coding, graphics design, the addition of content, and site operation. The accounting for website development varies, depending upon the stage of completion of the project. The relevant accounting is:

- *Stage 1: Preliminary.* Charge all site planning costs to expense as incurred. This stage is considered to include project planning, the determination of site functionality, hardware identification, technology usability, alternatives analysis, supplier demonstrations, and legal considerations.
- *Stage 2: Application development and infrastructure.* The accounting matches what was just described in the last section for internal-use software. In essence, capitalize these costs. More specifically, capitalize the cost of obtaining and registering an Internet domain, as well as the procurement of software tools, code customization, web page development, related hardware, hypertext link creation, and site testing. Also, if a site upgrade provides new functions or features to the website, capitalize these costs.
- *Stage 3: Graphics development.* For the purposes of this topic, graphics are considered to be software and so are capitalized, unless they are to be marketed externally. Graphics development includes site page design and layout.
- *Stage 4: Content development.* Charge data conversion costs to expense as incurred, as well as the costs to input content into a website. Content may include articles, photos, maps, charts, and so forth.
- *Stage 5: Site operation.* The costs to operate a website are the same as any other operating costs, and so should be charged to expense as incurred. Operating costs relate to training, administration, site updates, site security, and maintenance. The treatment of selected operating costs associated with a website are:
  - Charge website hosting fees to expense over the period benefited by the hosting
  - Charge search engine registration fees to expense as incurred, since they are advertising costs

Film Costs

Film costs are initially classified as an asset. This asset is comprised of a number of different costs, which are as follows:

- *Film rights.* This is the cost incurred to acquire the rights to a book or screenplay, which can then be adapted to film.
- *Production overhead.* This is an allocation of the costs of those people or departments with significant responsibility for film production. The overhead classification does not include general and administrative expenses.

- *Significant changes to a film.* This is the cost incurred to add significant additional content, such as a scene reshoot, to a film.
- *Episodic television series.* The costs associated with an episodic television series are capitalized, but only to the extent of the expected revenue. Any costs incurred in excess of this amount for each episode are to be charged to expense as incurred. Any costs charged to expense in this manner cannot later be capitalized into film costs.

An overall rule that applies to the allocation of costs to films is that costs cannot be allocated to a film if they have already been charged to expense.

Record Master Costs

A record company will incur costs to produce a record master, which is the master tape generated from the performance of an artist. The record company can record these costs as an asset, as long as the past performance and current popularity of the artist provides a sound basis for estimating the extent to which the cost will be recovered from future sales. When this is not the case, the record master cost should be charged to expense.

Summary

Of the intangible assets described in this chapter, the ones most likely to result in a recognized intangible asset are internally-developed software for internal use and website development costs (the other assets described here only relate to the entertainment industry). In both cases, only certain types of costs related to particular activities can be capitalized, with all other costs being charged to expense as incurred. This means that the accounting department will need to be routinely involved in the recordation of costs for both of these activities, to ensure that costs are capitalized in accordance with the rules set forth by the accounting standards.

Chapter 8
Valuation Issues for Specific Asset Types

Introduction

In this chapter, we cover valuation issues relating to certain common types of intangible assets. These issues cover two main topics, which are the types of assets that fall within each category and the circumstances under which the various valuation approaches can be applied to them.

The Valuation of Computer Software and Data

There are several ways to develop a valuation for computer software. It may have value because it can be copyrighted, or patented, or treated as a trade secret. Furthermore, if it is being developed for sale to others, then the software may have a trade name associated with it. A business may also be able to assign a value to its database of business information, covering such areas as customer, supplier, inventory, and accounting data. Furthermore, if a business is involved in a manufacturing process, then its database of process information may have value, covering such matters as unit flows and production pressures and temperatures by machine. It may also be possible to assign a value to the user manuals and training documentation associated with an organization's computer systems, when they have been developed internally.

The cost approach to valuation can be applied to computer software and data when it has been purchased from an outside party, or when it was developed internally and there is no market for its sale or licensing outside of the business. If these systems were developed in-house, then the cost approach will involve estimating the amount of development work required; this may call for an estimate of the number of lines of code to be written, multiplied by an average software developer labor rate per line. A charge for depreciation and obsolescence is then deducted from the compiled cost.

When software has been purchased from outside the company, then the most appropriate valuation approach is a market valuation. Since the provider has likely sold the software to a number of other parties, it should be relatively easy to obtain market prices for similar sales that can be used for a valuation.

In cases where software has been developed for sale or licensing to third parties, the income approach can be used to estimate future income – which can then be capitalized into a valuation for the software.

When working with any of these valuation methods, there are several issues that may impact the valuation. First, consider the age of the underlying code, the generation of the software language in which the code is written, and the level of obsolescence of the software or the hardware on which the software runs. If the answer to any of these issues is "old," then it can negatively impact the valuation. Also, a low level of program and/or system documentation can reduce the value of the software, since it would be harder to replicate or use. Further, a high level of excess, redundant, or duplicate code in the software can reduce its value, since they are indicative of software obsolescence.

The Valuation of Contracts

A contract is an agreement between two parties, which lays out their rights and obligations. It may require them to take a certain action, or not to do so. There are many types of contracts, including ones with suppliers, customers, employees, franchisees, and government entities. The specific terms of each agreement will drive its valuation. The contract types most commonly valued under the cost approach are licenses, franchises, employee contracts, operating licenses, and permits.

An expected contract renewal can be considered an intangible asset. For example, a contract that is expected to be renewed for an additional three-year term may have significant value, especially if its terms generate a notable amount of profit. In this situation, the analyst may value the original contract separately from the expected contract, or value them as a single unit.

Before attempting a contract valuation, you should first consider whether the contract is legally enforceable, the extent to which it can be enforced, the specific terms allowing it to be extended, whether it contains a schedule of payments, and whether it allows for liquidation damages. All of these factors impact the value of the contract.

The cost method may be used to value a contract. This typically involves a compilation of the direct and indirect costs incurred to negotiate it. Or, if the contract is a license, then the relevant costs are those incurred to apply for the license. Indirect costs may include legal, consulting, and engineering fees.

If the market approach is used, it is usually limited to the prices at which similar licenses, permits, and franchises are being sold in the most relevant market. Most contracts fall outside of this limited area.

If the income approach is used, the valuation should be based on the income specifically associated with a contract.

The Valuation of Customer Assets

At its most basic level, a customer asset is comprised of the contact information for all customers. This is only an indicator of the underlying customer relationships, but is still an asset. At a deeper level, the customer asset is comprised of records about the individual transactions that the business has had with its customers, which may indicate whether certain customers respond well to discount offers, and which ones make purchases irrespective of such offers. These records are needed to maintain in-depth relations with customers. An additional layer of customer asset is the firm's expectations for future sales to its existing customer base. This may include sales forecasts for specific products and services with individual customers. These three layers comprise the full range of value associated with the customer asset.

Many organizations have no trouble valuing their customer list asset, because they routinely license it as a mailing list to other organizations. For example, a credit card company might sell its customer mailing list to an investment advisory firm, which needs contact information for individuals with very large-dollar spending habits. The valuation task is more difficult for the complete database of customer information, which businesses do not usually license out. Instead, it is maintained solely for the company's own use.

The main intangible asset of many service-related businesses is its customer relationships. These entities have a detailed knowledge of their customers, the products they like to purchase, and how best to contact them. Without these relationships, these firms might very well go out of business. These customer relationships might have taken many years to acquire, and so are considered the most essential asset in the business. This asset is not necessarily based on identifiable customer contracts – only on the expectation that existing relationships will result in additional customer business over time.

All three valuation methods can be applied to customer assets. The market approach is certainly applicable when there is a history of licensing customer information to third parties. For example, if a competing bank licenses its customer contact list for $1 per name, then this is good data upon which to build a valuation. When such external licensing data is not available, it is more common to use a cost-based valuation, which focuses on the time required to replace the information in a firm's customer database. Or, if the valuation is targeted at an organization's customer relationships, then a better approach might be an income-based valuation. This involves estimating the future cash flows to be gained from customers, discounted to their present value. These future cash flows are reduced over time to reflect the likely decline in the organization's existing customer base as the years go by.

No matter what method is used to value customer assets, there are a number of factors to be considered when devising a valuation. For example, how difficult would it be to transfer these assets to a new owner? A low level of friction would indicate that the asset is more valuable. Or, how much difficulty would customers have in shifting their business elsewhere? If it is difficult to do so, then those customers will be more likely to keep buying from the firm for a long period of time. Another consideration is the frequency with which those customers buy from the firm. If purchases are frequent, then it has more opportunities to build relations with them. Yet another issue is the rate of change in revenue generated from the average customer. If this rate of change is increasing over time, then the customers are more valuable. Finally, a major consideration is the rate of customer turnover. Low turnover is exceedingly valuable, since it implies that the company has to invest less money in marketing to attract new customers, which increases its profits. The importance of these factors will vary, depending on the type of customer and the industry in which the organization does business.

The Valuation of Employee-Related Assets

There are several types of intangible assets related to the employees of a business, of which the most common are employee contracts. Here are several examples:

- *Employment agreements*. These agreements state the rights and obligations of both parties, where the employer gains the specialized services of the employee, while the employee gains a specific compensation and benefit arrangement.

- *Performance agreements*. These agreements are usually between professional athletes and sports teams, guaranteeing player services in exchange for a certain amount of compensation. These agreements usually constitute a large part of the value of a sports team.
- *Noncompetition agreements*. These agreements prevent employees from competing directly against the employer for a certain period of time, and possibly within a specific geographic region.
- *Endorsement agreements*. These agreements are usually between well-known individuals and the purveyors of goods or services, who pay these people for their product endorsements.

It is also possible to have an employee-related intangible asset that is not supported by contracts. This is an organization's assembled workforce. The value of the assembled workforce is derived from its ability to conduct work in an efficient manner, based on their collective experience and expertise. Having such employees on staff is a significant asset, since otherwise the firm would have to constantly hire and train new employees, which would greatly decrease its operational abilities. Having an assembled workforce also reduces the risk of the employer, since the existing staff should be sufficiently well-trained to avoid most ongoing risks to which the business would be subjected.

The cost method may be used to derive the value of a firm's assembled workforce. This involves estimations of what it would cost to recruit, hire, and train an entirely new workforce for the business. Or, for employment agreements, the income approach may be used. Under the income approach, the analyst calculates the income derived from the services of an employee who has entered into an employment agreement, and then subtracts out the compensation to be paid to that person (as stated in the agreement). The resulting differential between the two figures (presumably a profit) can then be capitalized to arrive at the value of the agreement.

The Valuation of Engineering Assets

Some aspects of an organization's engineering operations can be considered intangible assets – namely, its engineering drawings and related technical documentation for products and processes. These assets are intended to document technology in sufficient detail for it to be transferred to a new owner or licensed to a third party. Examples of engineering intangible assets are product, process, and construction engineering drawings, blueprints, and specifications. In addition, engineering manuals concerning how equipment should be operated or maintained can also be considered an intangible asset. In essence, anything that can be used to create a machine, product, process, or building can be classified as an engineering intangible asset.

Note: The cost of an engineering drawing does not include the time required to invent the underlying product or process – only to properly document it.

It can be difficult to apply the market approach to the valuation of engineering assets, since there are rarely any comparable sales or licensing deals involving such assets in the marketplace. A better option is the cost approach, where the analyst determines what it would cost to replace these assets. When conducting a cost analysis, be sure to investigate obsolescence, since there is a good chance that the related products or processes are becoming functionally obsolete. It may be possible to apply the income approach to a valuation, but only if there is a discernible incremental amount of income directly associated with the asset in question. For example, the level of process throughput may be higher, or production costs lower, specifically because of an engineering asset. If so, these profit enhancements can be capitalized to yield an asset valuation.

The Valuation of Intellectual Property

Intellectual property is generally considered to consist of copyrights, patents, trade secrets, and trademarks. This property may be recognized as assets when a business combination occurs. If one of these asset types is routinely licensed, then the most applicable valuation method may be the market valuation approach. Or, the income approach may be applied if the property generates income for the owner (as would be the case for a film library). In the quite likely event that the property merely contributes to the value of the overall business, then the cost approach should be used instead to value it. The cost approach is commonly applied to the valuation of trade secrets, internally-developed software, training manuals, customer files, and related items.

It is reasonable to expect that the value of a patent or copyright will be greatest right after it has been granted. This is because the holder can be assured of a number of years of protection, where no one else can use the patented or copyrighted asset. However, as the legal expiration date approaches, the value of these assets will gradually decline, to the point where they have no value at all as of the expiration date.

The Valuation of Licenses

A *license* is the formal permission of a government entity to engage in a specific activity, or a private agreement to use some type of intellectual property. For example, an accountant is granted a license by his or her state board of accountancy to practice as a certified public accountant. Or, a business is licensed to manufacture vaccines by the Food and Drug Administration. As yet another example, a restaurant is granted a license to sell liquor on the premises. These licenses can be an extremely valuable intangible asset, especially when a business is forced to stop its operations if it loses a license, or if it grants exclusive rights to the business (essentially creating a monopoly).

The value of a license will depend in part on the extent to which it is granted within an industry. For example, if many people are granted CPA licenses, then this may not be sufficient to restrict the amount of CPA supply in an area, so that prices do not increase. Another valuation issue is how long a license lasts, and whether or not it can be renewed. If a license is continually being re-bid with the government, then it is of less value than one that is automatically renewed. Also, a license is more valuable if the party possessing it is allowed to sell it to another party.

Licenses are generally valued using the income approach. The analyst calculates how much the business is likely to generate in sales because of its license ownership, from which all related operating expenses are subtracted. The resulting (presumed) profit is then capitalized to derive the value of the license. The forecasting period used for this analysis would be limited to the term of the license, unless there are only minor procedural issues interfering with its renewal.

In cases where licenses can be freely traded, it may also be possible to apply the market approach to their valuation. For example, if there is a vibrant market for the purchase of taxi medallions, then the analyst could use recent transactions as the basis for a valuation for a taxi medallion in the same market.

Summary

A major takeaway from this chapter is that you do not have to use the same valuation approach for all intangible assets. Instead, the method chosen will depend on the asset type, how it is used, the availability of market information, and whether it directly generates any income. It is quite likely that a mix of valuation approaches will be used to develop the most accurate valuations for the full range of an organization's intangible assets.

Glossary

A

Active market. A market in which there is a sufficiently high volume of transactions to provide ongoing pricing information.

C

Copyright. The exclusive legal right to print, publish, perform, film, or record literary, artistic, or musical material.

Cost approach. A valuation method that uses the estimated cost to replace an asset (or the capabilities of the asset), adjusted for the obsolescence of the existing asset.

D

Developer's profit. The return a developer expects on funds invested in the development process for an asset.

Direct costs. The costs of labor, materials, and overhead directly incurred by the creator of an asset.

E

Entrepreneurial incentive. The opportunity cost of the creator of an intangible asset.

Entry price. The price at which an entity acquires an asset or assumes a liability.

Exit price. The price at which an entity sells an asset or pays a third party to take on a liability.

Expected cash flows. A probability-weighted average of several possible future cash flows.

External obsolescence. A decline in the value of an intangible asset, which is caused by external events.

F

Fair value. The estimated price at which an asset can be sold or a liability settled in an orderly transaction to a third party under current market conditions.

Fair value hierarchy. The different classes in which accounting standards classify inputs to a fair value measurement.

Functional obsolescence. When an asset can no longer perform the function(s) for which it was originally intended.

G

GAAP. Generally accepted accounting principles.

Glossary

Goodwill. The difference between the price paid for an acquiree and the fair value of all assets and liabilities of the acquiree that were purchased as part of the business combination.

H

Highest and best use. When fair value is determined based on the price at which an asset could theoretically be employed in its highest and best use, rather than the use in which the asset is currently employed.

I

Income approach. A valuation method that uses estimated future cash flows or earnings, adjusted by a discount rate that represents the time value of money and the risk of cash flows not being achieved, to derive a discounted present value.

Indirect costs. The costs of labor, materials, and overhead indirectly incurred by the creator of an asset.

Intangible assets. Assets that have no physical substance, where their value is derived from their associated legal rights.

L

License. The formal permission of a government entity to engage in a specific activity, or a private agreement to use some type of intellectual property.

M

Market approach. A valuation method that uses the prices associated with actual market transactions for similar or identical assets to derive a fair value.

Market price. The most likely price at which an asset would be sold in an open market.

Most advantageous market. The market in which the best price can be obtained, net of transaction costs.

O

Observable inputs. Inputs derived from market data that properly reflect the assumptions that third parties would use when setting prices for assets.

P

Patent. An authorization securing for a term of years the right to exclude others from making, using, or selling an invention.

Present value. The current worth of cash to be received or spent in the future, which has been discounted at a market rate of interest.

R

Relief from royalty method. The royalty rate that an organization would otherwise have to pay a third party to use a similar intangible asset.

Replacement cost new. The cost that would be incurred to create an asset with the same utility level of the current asset.

Reproduction cost new. The cost that would be incurred to create a duplicate of an asset as of the analysis date.

S

Service mark. A legally registered name or designation used in the manner of a trademark to distinguish an organization's services from those of its competitors.

T

Tangible asset. Any asset from which its value is derived from the use of its physical attributes.

Trade dress. The design and shape of the materials in which a product is packaged.

Trade secret. A secret device or technique used to manufacture products.

Trademark. A symbol, word, or words that are legally registered as representing a business or product.

Index

www.ingramcontent.com/pod-product-compliance
Lightning Source LLC
Chambersburg PA
CBHW080721220326
41520CB00056B/7346